Pottery's Perspective for Beginners

The Ultimate Guide, History, Getting Started, Inspiration of Pottery

Copyright © 2020

All rights reserved.

DEDICATION

The author and publisher have provided this e-book to you for your personal use only. You may not make this e-book publicly available in any way. Copyright infringement is against the law. If you believe the copy of this e-book you are reading infringes on the author's copyright, please notify the publisher at: https://us.macmillan.com/piracy

Contents

THE HISTORY OF POTTERY 1
HOW TO GET STARTED 11
    CHOOSING YOUR POTTERY CLAY – BEST POTTERY CLAY FOR BEGINNERS 12
    EQUIPMENT & TOOLS NEEDED TO GET STARTED 25
POTTERY INSPIRATION 32
POTTERY TIPS FOR BEGINNERS 41

The History of Pottery

Sometime between 6,000 and 4,000 BC, the first potter's wheel was invented in Mesopotamia. This brought about a revolution in the way ancient people could create items out of clay. No longer were pottery makers restricted to the long process of hand molding clay — they were then able to have more freedom in experimenting with new forms and aesthetics.

While pottery had always had intrinsic artistic qualities, when the potter's wheel arrived, it shifted the process even more. Instead of serving utilitarian purposes, it now served artistic ones. While the earliest types of items found by archaeologists were generally undecorated, unglazed, hand-formed clay vessels, by 6000 BC, places like the Middle East, China and Europe had developed a wide array of design techniques.

From intricate painted designs that told the history of a Pharaoh's reign to highly polished bowls and plates to elaborate animal figures, ceramists attained remarkable skill and ability that was never seen before, thanks to the invention of the potter's wheel.

If you want to know more about this unique, ancient practice and how it has evolved into the industry it is today, we've developed this guide for you. So, let's get started – here's the ultimate guide to the history of pottery!

1. What is Pottery?

Before we dive into the history of pottery, let's actually define what pottery is and how it's made.

Pottery is made up of ceramic materials and encompasses major types of pottery wares such as earthenware, stoneware and porcelain. To be considered pottery, a piece must be a fired ceramic ware that contains clay when formed.

To create a piece of pottery, the potter must form a ceramic/clay body into a specific object, whether by hand built or wheel thrown techniques, and then heat it at a high temperature in a kiln to remove water from the clay. This allows for changes in the molded object, increasing its strength and durability while permanently setting its shape.

The potter can decorate the clay body either before or after firing, however, some processes require the clay go through certain preparations in order to successfully create a piece of work. With kneading, a process which involves massaging the clay with your hands, it allows moisture within the clay to spread throughout the entire slab. When done correctly the clay will have even moisture content and you're one step away from creating.

The next preparatory procedure when working with clay is called de-airing. This is accomplished either by a vacuum machine that is attached to a pugmill or manually through the process of wedging. When the clay has been de-aired and de-moisturized, it's ready to be shaped in a variety of ways. Once it's shaped, it's dried and then fired.

2. What do you think it is about making pottery that resonates with people so much?

Pottery has been around since the ancient people roamed the earth. As one of the oldest human inventions, the practice of pottery has developed alongside civilization. The earliest ceramic objects have been dated as far back as 29,000 BC. One of the most popular pieces dated from this time period is The Venus of Dolni Vestonice, discovered in the Czech Republic, a ceramic Venus figurine of a nude female.

Since clay is found nearly everywhere, early humans had easy access to this responsive material, allowing them to mold and shape the world they observed around them. With limited access to tools, clay also let these people mold and shape by hand, creating human statuettes, bowls, utensils and more.

As soon as early humans developed fire, they discovered that heating these formed clay objects transformed them into a different material that was permanent and much more useful to them — mainly items like bowls, plates, and utensils for storing and preparing food.

As civilization made more advances, pottery has always advanced right alongside it, even assisting by helping people survive and providing them with a higher standard of living.

For example, about 21,000 years ago, people located in East Asia were hit with an exceptionally cold climate over a lengthy period of time. To survive, these ancient people had to obtain the maximum calorific and nutritional value from their food. Pottery was the solution. By creating pots, they could then cook their food and improve nutrient intake from starchy plants and meat, the common foods located in the area.

Because of its many utilitarian uses, pottery has been revered throughout history. Of course, over the centuries, it has developed into so much more than just functional ceramic items.

3. When was pottery production revolutionized?

Sometime between 6,000 and 4,000 BC, the first potter's wheel was invented in Mesopotamia. This brought about a revolution in the way ancient people could create items out of clay. No longer were pottery makers restricted to the long process of hand molding clay — they were then able to have more freedom in experimenting with new forms and aesthetics.

While pottery had always had intrinsic artistic qualities, when the potter's wheel arrived, it was a game changer! Instead of serving primarily utilitarian purposes, it branched out and shifted to embrace artistic expression. While the earliest types of items found by archaeologists were generally undecorated, unglazed, hand-formed clay vessels, by 6000 BC, places like the Middle East, China and Europe had developed a wide array of design techniques.

From intricate painted designs that told the history of a Pharaoh's reign to highly polished bowls and plates to elaborate animal figures, ceramists attained remarkable skill and ability that was never seen before, thanks to the invention of the potter's wheel.

4. How did potters wheels turn before electricity?

The first mechanical potter's wheel wasn't invented until the 19th century, so the first manual potter's wheel was truly a lasting innovation.

There are many ways to operate a potters wheel without electricity. For the most part, in ancient times, pottery wheels were turned manually, with the user kicking their feet to put it in motion. Other ways to spin a potters wheel included using a stick that is put in a hole at the top of the wheel and then turning it, or simply speeding it up by hand.

Once the mechanical wheel was invented, potters could start manufacturing multiple items per hour, completely revolutionizing the industry once again!

5. How has the making of pottery changed in the past 100 years?

Pottery has changed a lot since the early days of hand-formed ceramic bowls and manual wheels. The biggest change within the past 100 years involves the kiln, another required tool of the pottery trade. Since potter's wheels have been electrified, so too have kilns moved from gas to electric. Even in the past 20 years, innovators have made progress in the kiln industry, developing electronic programmers to control the temperature and power of the kiln.

When it comes to industrial production, fired ceramic ware has moved from jiggering to pressing. Jiggering is the mechanical adaptation of wheel throwing and is used where mass production or duplication of the same shape, like bowls and plates, is required. Pressing, on the other hand, involves setting a ceramic slab against a mold plate to achieve a customized look.

And some of the biggest innovators in today's pottery industry have taken a technologically focused approach. Most production lines at major manufacturing facilities have been automated to reduce human power while increasing machine automation.

6. What do you think the greatest advantage is to producing pottery?

Pottery is one of the most durable forms of art, with many fragments found from almost all time periods and civilizations throughout the world. There's no doubt that ceramic items last much longer than other artifacts that were crafted from less-durable materials. When a person makes a piece of pottery, they're likely to consider it's lasting quality and what it means to have something made by their hands be found millenniums later — it's something that piques the interest of many who learn the practice.

Within the studios of Deneen Pottery, many resident potters say this is the reason they got into the work in the first place. When asked about the longevity of this unique medium, Texas Teena, art director of Deneen Pottery responded, "I think of that often, especially when I design a ceramic mug that has a historic building on it. There could come a time when the only our mug is the only remaining reproduction of that building."

7. What is the most exciting thing that has happened to pottery within the last five years?

Thanks to the intersection of pottery customization, marketing and affordability, more and more people are snatching up custom-design items, like branded coffee mugs. From corporations and nonprofits to museums and monuments, even events; everyone wants to take advantage of the many benefits a custom-designed mug offers, making it a hot-selling item for pottery companies around the world.

Pottery's Perspective for Beginners

How to Get Started

Making pottery for beginners can be an enjoyable, therapeutic and relatively easy hobby to pick up. Almost anyone can grow their skills as a potter with the right tools, techniques and inspiration.

Just because you're a beginner, you should never be afraid to get started creating gorgeous, hand-thrown or hand-built pottery. If you're trying to learn the art, we've developed this guide for you. So let's get started – here's the ultimate guide on how to get started with pottery!

Choosing Your Pottery Clay – Best Pottery Clay For Beginners

Before considering what equipment to buy, it's worth thinking about what clay to use. There are many different clays you can choose from. Find out which one is best for you.

What to Look For When Selecting Clay

1) Type of Clay Body (Earthenware, Stoneware, or Porcelain)

2) Texture (Smooth, course, or in-between)

3) Cone size (Firing Temperature)

4) Color (What effect are you looking for)

5) Price (Good Price Point for beginners)

1) What Type of Clay Body To Use

The difference in types of clay has to do with the different minerals, the amount of plasticity (Stickiness and workability), the size of the platelets, and the firing temperatures.

There are 3 basics types of clay for beginners to choose from; Earthenware, Stoneware, and Porcelain. These are a few things you will want to know when choosing your clay.

Qualities of Earthenware

This is a good clay for throwing on wheel and handbuilding because it's easy to work with and shape.

It is very porous, that's why it is used for flowerpots, bricks and other outdoor construction. If it freezes, water can't get trapped inside and crack.

You can make almost anything with earthenware. If you want it to be watertight and food-safe, just glaze it, and hand wash only.

This clay is basically a low-fire clay. Most Earthenware is bisque fired at Cone 04 1945 °F (1063 °C) and Glaze Fired at cone 05 1888 °F or 1031 °C. or Cone 06 1828 °F or 998 °C.

It is commonly made thicker because it chips easier than other clay types.

Is typically red or orange (terracotta) because of its high content of iron oxide, but you can also find it in white.

Is more durable and chip-resistant than earthenware and which makes it more popular in its use for dinnerware and mugs.

You can make almost anything with stoneware depending on how much sand or grog is added.

Their colors range from white, buff (sand), brown, and different shades of gray.

It is a lower quality clay than porcelain but more popular because of its durability and value.

Stoneware has two firing temperatures: Mid fire range which is typically Cone 5 2167 °F (1186 °C) to Cone 6 2232 °F (1222 °C). And High fire which is usually Cone 10 2345 °F (1285 °C).

It's better for beginner potters because we tend to play with our clay far longer than the pros. Highly recommend these Clays. Amaco Stoneware #46, Buff Clay (amazon) – (blick arts) or (walmart) because it holds up nicely even without sand or grog in it. If you prefer a white clay check out Amaco stoneware 38 (amazon) – (blick arts) or (walmart) is also a good choice

Qualities of Porcelain

True porcelain feels smooth as butter and less forgiving than other clays.

It absorbs water rather quickly which can make big changes in its workability.

When it comes to pottery or ceramics, porcelain is known to be the most regal of all clay types.

These porcelains are not the true porcelains, but I still find them to be nice clays to throw with.

You can also get mid to high fire porcelain. Mid fire range which is typically Cone 5 2167 °F (1186 °C) to Cone 6 2232 °F (1222 °C). And High fire which is usually Cone 10 2345 °F (1285 °C).

When this type of clay starts to collapse it's hard to get it back, but oh so smooth to play with on the wheel. It's totally worth the challenge.

2) What Is The Best Texture For You

A good thing to know when selecting your clay is if there is grog (ground up fired clay), sand, both, or none in your clay. Your selection will depend on what you are using your clay for and what skill level you are.

Handbuilding Clay

When handbuilding you want to have a good amount of grog or sand in your clay. There are several reasons for this:

You need a clay that has the ability to stand on its own as you create your masterpiece.

While scoring and slipping pieces together, you don't want your clay to start slumping or even collapse.

When choosing a handbuilding clay, it's best to go with one that has more grog, sand, or both, because it's better to have a lower shrinkage rate to help prevent cracking.

Clay For Throwing On The Wheel

You will want your clay to be as smooth as possible without collapsing on the wheel.

When it comes to throwing clay on the wheel, porcelain truly is the best.

3) What Cone Size Do You Need

To What Temperature Will You Fire?

You want the cone size of your clay to match the cone size of your glazes because clay and glaze can expand and contract together making them an exact fix and food safe. There are basically three different temperature ranges. When buying your clay, it's important to know what temperature the kiln will be firing to and the cone size of your clay body and glaze.

Lower fire ranges anywhere from Cone 022 (1087 degrees F) to Cone 2 (2088 degrees F) Most popular firing range is Cone 04 to 06.

Note: Low firing pottery will not be waterproof unless it is glazed.

Mid fire ranges between Cone 3 (2106 degrees F) to Cone 7 (2,262 degrees F) Most popular fire range is Cone 5 and 6.

Mid-fire is popular because of the numerous colors of glazes to choose from, plus being dinnerware safe. When choosing your mid-fire clay make sure it does NOT have a zero in front of the number. If the clay or glaze is low fire it will melt in the kiln.

High fire ranges from Cone 8 (2280 degrees F) to Cone 10 (2,345 degrees F) most popular is Cone 10.

This clay is stronger and durable than lower fired clays. If the clay you high fire is mid-fire only or low-fire it will melt in the kiln.

4) Colors To Choose From

The great part about buying clay today is the array of colors you have to choose from. These are some colors you may want to consider.

White is a nice choice if you want your glaze colors to pop. The color tends to turn out more vibrant. Clean up is also better because white clay does not stain your clothes or anything else for that matter.

Sand/ Buff color is very close to white when it comes to glazes being vibrant because there's not much of a difference. When buff clay is wet it looks pretty dark, once it is bisque it has a nice light buff color that doesn't interfere with the glaze colors.

Red is great if you like working with a deep, rich color. Red is beautiful with a clear matte, satin, or glossy glaze over it. Darker clays will stain your clothes because of the iron content in them. Check out What to wear when making pottery.

Black clay is a stunning color that goes beautifully with light or white underglazes or all by its self with a clear glaze.

Make your own color. Another fun part of clay is being able to mix powdered colorants into your clay to create an array of different colored clays. You can even put strips of white and colored clay together to create a marble effect when you throw it on the wheel.

Each color is beautiful in its own way depending on what look you want to achieve.

5) Price Point

The great part about clays today is the selections you have and the range of prices to choose from. As a beginner, I would start out with the lower-priced clay because of the sheer amount of practice clay you will go through.

Another way to save some money and show a little love to your clay is to recycle or reclaim your scrap clay.

There are wonderful clays in the mid-range price and there are high-quality, high-end clays like the true porcelains that are so beautiful but not that forgiving.

Keep in mind you may have a local store in your area to save on shipping costs, or you could buy bulk. When you're on a roll, you would be surprised at how much clay you can go through.

In Conclusion

Keep this list in mind when choosing your clay to help you make the best choice. Knowing what you need and want in your pottery clay makes all the difference in the world. It's a good idea to practice with different clays until you find the one that feels right for you.

If you want to know about more clay info and choices, then check out my Top Clay Picks page.

A Few More Related Questions

Is it Better To Buy Dry Or Moist Clay

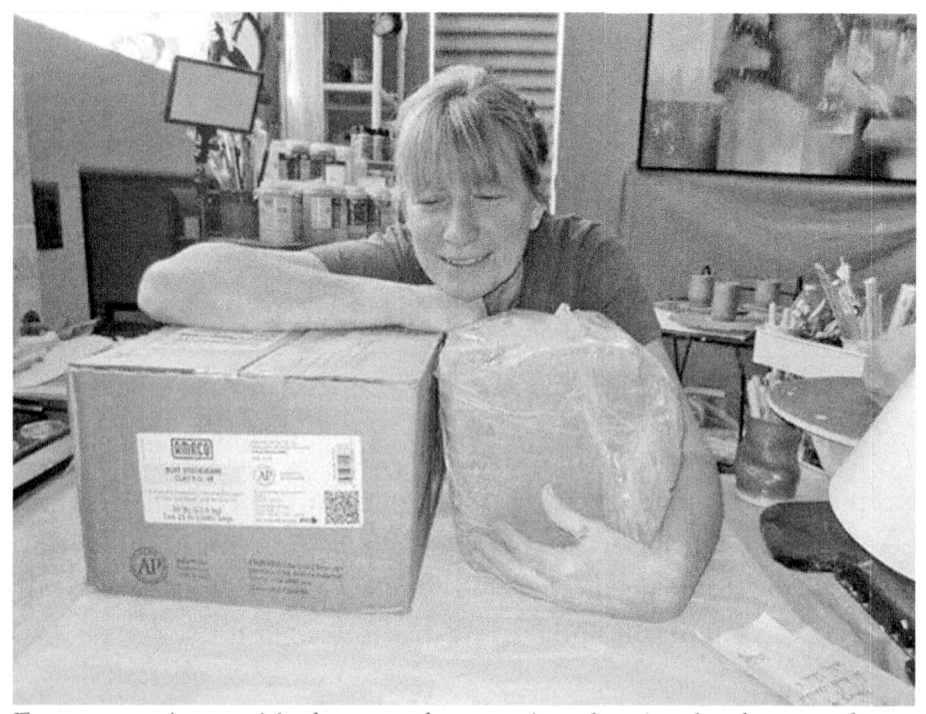

For convenience, it's best to buy moist clay in the bag ready to wedge.

There are some definite advantages to buying dry clay such as the shipping cost, weight, storage, and mixing it to your own liking with the right amount of sand, grog or other minerals. Mixing Dry clay has some extra steps and there is a definite learning curve, this is why a Beginner Potter should always get moist premade ready to wedge clay.

Can You Mix Different Clays Together

Most beginners don't know enough about how different clays will interact with each other. Plus, there are different shrinkage rates in each clay. If the shrinkage rate is not the same, then the clay particles will shrink at different rates putting pressure on the platelets. This could cause your mixed clay to crack as it dries. If you have several different clays it's best to keep them separate and mark our bags and containers.

What Is The Best Clay For Cookies

A cookie is made by rolling out your clay a quarter-inch thick like a sheet of cookie dough; then cut circles out that look like cookies and bisque them. Cookies are used to prevent the Glaze from running on to your Kiln shelf by placing them under your glazed pieces. Make sure the cookie is larger than the base of your piece to catch that runaway glaze.

When Glazing Pottery, it's best to use cookies especially if you're a beginner.

The best clay to use for cookies would be a Cone 10 Stoneware with Heavy Grog. There are several reasons for this.

Cone 10 can withstand high heat. If you are low-firing or mid-firing, your cookie will last longer. After all, you don't want to be making cookies all the time. (unless they are the eating kind.)

Stoneware is stronger and therefore will last longer.

Heavy grog also makes your cookie stronger, plus it makes your shrinkage rate a lot less. This is important because you don't want your cookie to shrink under your glazed piece.

If you use this clay for your cookies, they will last many glaze firings, and you don't have to make them as often.

Equipment & Tools Needed To Get Started

Before going out and buying anything, see if there are any evening classes or courses in your area. If you get the bug for mud, then you can start thinking about getting your own setup.

Methods of producing pottery for beginners

There are many different methods of producing ceramics. Some people make beautiful professional pottery from rolled out slabs of clay. Slabs can be formed into cylinders or slumped over molds to form plates or bowls. Slabs of clay can be rolled by hand, or if many are required a slab roller machine can be used.

Pottery can be cast in molds using a runny wet mix of clay called slip.

Molds can be bought from ceramic supply stores, or made from plaster if a special design is required.

A pottery wheel can also be used to throw clay into many shapes. It does take time to learn the throwing skill, but once mastered it's a very efficient method. Pottery wheels can be electric or powered by the potter kicking their leg.

Pottery for beginners equipment list

The main piece of equipment necessary is a kiln. If you are only interested in ornaments or models you could use polymer clay or air drying stuff. If you are interested in making any tableware, vases or other robust pottery a kiln is vital. Some potters use wood or gas to fire kilns. For this article I'll concentrate on electric kilns as they are more suitable for pottery for beginners. Most small electric kilns fire to a max temp of around 1280°C.

Buying a kiln for the first time

The smallest kilns will be more mobile and can plug into a standard mains socket. Larger kilns may need to be wired into the mains by an electrician. Smaller kilns mean firings can be done more often. It doesn't take as long to make enough pieces to fill the kiln to fire it efficiently.

The most important things to look for in a used kiln is the condition of the firebricks, and the elements. Usually there will be some ware and tear with a used kiln. However, major cracks in the lid or base, or elements hanging out of the bricks should raise alarm bells. Kilns wear out over time, each firing degrades the elements which will eventually need replacing.

Buying a new kiln is much like a new car, you get something shiney and fresh that you know hasn't been abused. Spending thousands wasn't really an option for me, and my kiln is still working well after four years occasional use.

Due to the extremely high temperatures, kilns need to be located in a garage or external building. Care should be taken to remove flammable materials from the area.

Choosing a potters wheel for beginners

Assuming you are interested in the throwing method of production, you will need a wheel. If space is limited an electric wheel would be more suitable. For a beginner potter even the smallest electric wheel would be sufficient. It's only when making really big pots that a high powered wheel is needed for more torque. Some wheels only have a gear system with a number of speed increments. The ability to reverse the wheel direction is important if you're someone who find it easier to throw the 'wrong way'.

People using kick wheels say they feel more in control than using electric wheels.

What potters tools are needed for beginners?

Not many too are needed when starting out. It's easy to get carried away when looking at a ceramics supply brochure or pottery website. The most important tools are your hands, and these should be looked after! The hands are actually great at producing natural curves on pots.

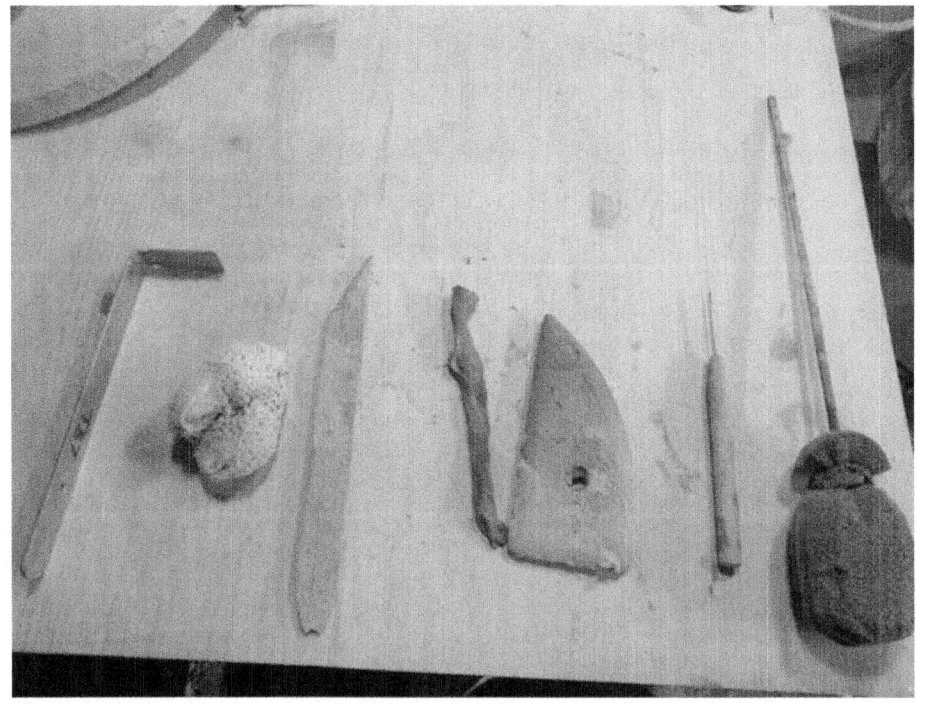

Top seven tools for pottery throwing!

The wire is usually nylon or metal with wooden toggles at each end to grab hold of.

A sponge is used to wet the pot with water while throwing to provide lubrication. A sponge on a stick is handy for removing water from inside narrow necked forms.

When making plates or shallow bowls a wooden rib is useful for smoothing the base.

Pin tools are great for cutting the top from wobbly pots, or popping air bubbles. Thin pin tools are better than the fatter ones.

A throwing stick can clean up the outside of pots, and make an undercut bevel at the base. A bevel makes cutting the pot from the wheel easier.

A trimming tool is needed if making pots with footrings. This tool is used to refine the shape when the clay has firmed up.

Glaze choices for pottery beginners

Some pottery such as flowerpots may be made without being glazed.

Most other pottery items are glazed. Glaze can be gloss or matte finish, with many levels between. Generally a gloss glaze is favoured for tableware due to its easily cleaned surface. Some glazes may be coloured but still show some of the clay body beneath. This may be good if using a speckled clay which you'd like to be seen.

The easiest way to make a glaze is to buy a ready made powder from a ceramics supplier. There are many options for colours when buying ready made glazes. Importantly the firing temperature must match that of your clay, and be within the limits of your kiln.

When trying out a new glaze 2kg of powder would be sufficient to enable dipping of mugs or other small items. As a starting point 1kg of water should be added per 1kg of powder. When working with any powdered glaze materials you should definitely wear a respirator mask. A fine sieve should be used to pass the mixed glaze and remove any large particles. Sieves are an essential for a good glaze finish, try and get an 80 mesh as a minimum. They are available from pottery supply places.

With so many other things to learn when starting in pottery, glaze chemistry could be a bridge too far.

Pottery Inspiration

For Décor

Pottery decor, whether it's a family heirloom or a fortuitous find, provides a space with visual intrigue that adds substance and soul to your overall home design.

For generations, pottery has served both functional and aesthetic purposes, and not much has changed in the modern world of today. From prehistoric food storage vessels to tiles on space shuttles to decorative flower pots in your bedroom, pottery plays a crucial role in a variety of ways.

Atwater Pottery

In general, the artistic role of pottery within the facet of home decor is growing. In all shapes and sizes, pottery is the perfect antidote to homogeneous decor. Whether displayed sparingly across a mantelpiece or a main component of a room's decor, pottery has staked its claim as a unique design accessory.

In this section of The Ultimate Guide to Pottery, we're exploring inspirational ways to utilize pottery within your home decor. Let's get started!

BEST PRACTICES: WAYS TO DISPLAY YOUR POTTERY

First, let's get some basics out of the way. Below are best practices on how to display your pottery for maximum effect.

Group pottery pieces by color. Even if you're going for a minimal, slimmed-down color scheme, you can still work pottery into your home's decor. In fact, pottery can provide a splash of color to add even more visual intrigue. When decorating your home with pottery, group pieces together by color in a primary location to minimize the "cluttered" feeling and promote a more intentional arrangement. Putting colored vessels against a neutral backdrop, or neutral vessels against a colored backdrop will make your interior design stand out more, elevating the grouping to an art piece that can be moved and changed at will.

However, you shouldn't be concerned with quantity over quality. To make a statement, you can have one gorgeous piece as the focal point of the room, complementing the color scheme to attract the eye toward the piece. Additionally, you can display several pieces from the same color family to draw-in attention.

Arrange pottery pieces artfully. Give smaller pottery pieces an anchor by including them in groupings with larger pieces. While it takes a good eye to properly mix shapes, experimentation is key. By keeping your groupings tight and placed purposefully toward one side of a surface — whether it's a mantle, built-in bookcase or credenza — you create a space in your room that feels curated over time rather than purchased all at once just to fill out the area.

Placing taller items toward the back and pieces with more volume in the center will provide the foundation for your display. Medium-sized pottery can be added to build support, with the smallest pieces filling the gaps and rounding out the display.

Promote an organic style with plants. One of the easiest ways to achieve an organic look and inject some color into your decor is to add plants to your pottery. Try adding flowers, houseplants and herbs in beautifully glazed pots that accent your overall interior design.

Choose pots that support the beauty of the plant rather than take away from it. They should also be wide and deep enough to allow the plant to grow properly. Speckled or dual glazes in soft tones, for example, are perfect for enhancing the look of a plant and pottery display without sacrificing other design elements in the room.

Know the different types of pottery. From pottery to ceramics to porcelain, there are many various types of pottery. Pottery is generally considered to be any container made of clay. Ceramics are made from clay and glaze that are permanently changed when heated. Porcelain is a strong, vitreous, translucent ceramic material that is bisque-fired at a low temperature, then glazed and fired again at a very high temperature.

FIT POTTERY WITHIN THE OVERALL HOME STYLE YOU WANT TO ACHIEVE

Everyone's home style is different. However, that doesn't mean you can't incorporate pottery into your home decor, whether you're going for a midcentury modern, rustic farmhouse, contemporary style or anything in between.

Midcentury modern style. This Scandinavian-inspired style has remained a popular choice for interior design enthusiasts since the 1950s. With its soft lines, uncomplicated textiles, low-profile furnishings and simple materials, midcentury modern is an attractive and attention-grabbing way to decorate your home's interior. This style also accommodates pottery as a huge part of the overall decor. Bright colors, interesting shapes and an almost endless array of styles allow for simple updates when it comes to implementing the perfect piece of pottery for this clean, popular aesthetic.

Rustic farmhouse style. For those DIY interior decorators that love a rustic farmhouse look, pottery is the perfect addition. The best pottery to support your rustic farmhouse design are hand-painted pieces. To make the most of pieces in vibrant shades, keep them together en masse. For any pieces that have an authentic, timeworn style, such as an antique hutch, hand-painted pottery provides the right counterpoint. Another way to make your pottery pieces stand out is to paint the back of the display case in a rich, complementary hue to showcase your pieces.

Contemporary style. When going for a contemporary style, pottery fits in well. With a well-pieced-together collection of pottery pieces, you can quickly warm up an otherwise empty space in a nontraditional way.

Vintage style. If vintage is the style you're trying to achieve, soft linens, feminine furnishings and accessories that tell stories most likely form the basis of your interior design. Adding in a hefty dose of cream-colored pottery keeps the look in-lined with a vintage style. Don't overdo it with large pieces; instead go for a variety of sizes and shapes to keep the pottery decor from falling to the wayside of other decor. If you want to add some formality, arrange your pottery behind glass doors but in plain view. Don't forget to run a duster over your pieces and display case once a month to keep everything clean and tidy!

Eclectic style. For an eclectic look, try using a variety of pottery in an arresting display of shapes and colors against a monochromatic paint color — light or dark — to add a twist to your space. Balance the feel of the collection by ensuring the scale of the surrounding furnishings, lighting and art are larger than the pottery. To stop your display from veering into hoarder territory, keep it constrained to just one shelf or flat surface.

Pottery Inspiration for Decor in Conclusion

With a few simple tips and guidelines, however, you can transform your space into a visually appealing one. From antique to modern hand-thrown vases, it can keep your space from feeling sterile or impersonal. Whether you're a minimalist who prefers a single piece or someone who prefers the look of a group of pottery pieces, there's a something special out there ready to be integrated into your overall home design. Best of luck with your decorating efforts!

Pottery Tips For Beginners

Benefits of choosing to work with pottery

Crafting beautiful pottery works from a lump of clay is not only a fun way of passing the time, but it also has got some health benefits. Let's have a look.

Activities	How does it help?
Creating something new	It helps you to imagine more and finally aids you to give your imagination a shape.
Focusing on something	Pottery is a task that is quite impossible to accomplish if you don't concentrate on it adequately. So, in this way, it improves your concentration.
Experimenting	The more you work with it, the more it helps you

and exploring	in experimenting and exploring something new and unique.
Kneading, twisting, and shaping	The more you knead and twist the clay lump with your hand, it works as an exercise to your hands, wrists, and fingers. Also, it works magically in reducing stress.

Pottery Tips and Tricks for Beginners

Despite the art of pottery having the afore-said benefits, some people refrain from opting for this art, thinking that it's a tough job. However, you must keep the fact in mind that once you become used to, with the tricks and techniques, there is no way of looking back. So, now we will provide a few pottery tips that can be useful for those who are willing to try their hands on this artwork for the first time.

Be comfy

One thing that you need to take care of when you go to your first pottery class or session is, wear comfortable clothes, not the stylish ones as you're going to deal with clay and create pottery. And if you wear stylish clothes, they can get stains, and you may end up ruining them. Hence, always take care of your comfort, not your style.

Don't expect to be amazing right away

Well, creating pottery pieces is not an easy task. It is an art that requires regular hard work and patience. You're not going to create amazing things right away; it will take time. The motions are often hard to duplicate the most when it comes to pottery. If you indulge in a pottery class, you will probably see your instructor throw the pottery like it's nothing.

However, it is not easy. The actual reason behind it is that they're doing it for so many years & they're used to doing it. So, never get frustrated and lose hope; keep trying and have some patience. Here are the key points that you should follow if you want to master the pottery:

- Keep your expectations low, especially in the beginning.
- The determination to learn one new thing each session
- Try to keep the frustrations at bay

If you go in with your expectations super high, such as you think you're going to end up throwing beautiful pieces right away, or you're going to be the next master of pottery, you're going to end up hating this beautiful art. You should go in with the idea that you want to do a little better than the last time, and even if it's just learning to move your hands a little bit in each direction a different way, you will definitely progress. However, it will take time, and if you keep doing hard work, you will definitely be going to achieve your goals.

Learn Clay Throwing Techniques

If you're really having trouble with pottery in the beginning, you should join a wheel-thrown pottery class. Find the pottery classes near you and choose the best one. While you can explore the internet and learn the techniques by reading articles or watching videos, but if you join a class, you will be able to meet the experts who can help you with their experience & your instructor will tell you about your mistakes and help you to get better at pottery.

Get proper knowledge of your equipment/ingredients:

Pottery work is nothing but all about following the correct tricks and techniques. While working with the supplies, you must become pretty familiar with the components. Without knowing the nature of the equipment with which you're going to work, you will never be able to get control over them properly. So, it's essential to know the traits of the ingredients or tools that you will be using.

- Clay: The soul material for crafting a pottery work is clay. So, you should know the nature of your clay first. There are different types of clays available in the market. So, it's quite tricky to choose the right one, especially if you're a beginner. For that, you need to become a good observer. Try to notice how much time your clay takes to get hardened, how much moisture is there in it, and how much moisture it absorbs to become workable enough. Here are some of the fundamental traits that you should look for in a good clay:
- Flexibility: The clay should be pliable enough so that it becomes easy to work with. The fine flexible texture allows you to knead, twist shape, and blend the clay the way you want.
- Less sticky: Your clay shouldn't become much sticky when you're adding some water into it. If it sticks too much to your hands, you're going to create nothing but a total mess, which is quite frustrating enough. So, it is crucial to choose a clay that is

not so sticky.
- Softness: Opt for a lump of clay that is quite soft, and gets your job done comfortably. While kneading and twisting, it doesn't become frustrating so that you can shape the clay with ease.
- Color of the clay: There are natural colors in clays that come from the essential minerals present in it. Such natural shades give your clay project a pleasant and beautiful color. While choosing the clay color, try to select the one that is compatible with your project and doesn't create any problem when you try to glaze it or paint it.
- Non-Toxic and Safe: As clays are natural properties of the Earth, it is non-toxic and environment-friendly. So, whether you're using it to make pots for your daily usage or any other purpose, make sure to opt for the clays that you're not allergic to or doesn't contain any harsh chemical. Choose the one that is safe to work with.
- Hardening nature: It is quite an important trait that you should observe in any clay. How much time your clay takes to get hardened, is vital for your pottery work, as it's going to decide the time factor of your project. Some clays need to be dried with heat or fire. Again, other types of clays automatically dry up when kept in normal air. Choose the right one according to your needs.
- Wheel: Wheel plays a vital role in shaping your clay. So make sure you have chosen the right pottery wheel for your work. What to look for in a potter's wheel? Here you go:
- Longevity: Before investing in your first pottery wheel, make sure it is durable enough that you need not compromise with

your pottery work at any cost.
- Configuration of the wheel head: Choose the dimension of your wheel head based on the size of the pottery you're going to make.
- Portability: Opt for a portable wheel, so that you can carry it to your suitable place easily.

To buy your first set of the pottery wheel, you can opt for SKYTOU Pottery Wheel Pottery Forming Machine and enjoy sculpting as much as you want.

Glaze: Glazing is an integral part of pottery. Though as a beginner, you need to become adept at shaping and sculpting more, there are no limitations if you want to start your glazing work at the beginning itself. For glazing, you need to keep the following things in your mind.

Ingredients of glazing: You should know about the type of glazing you're going to apply on your pottery piece. Whether you want to give it a glossy or shiny effect or a matte texture, you need to take the ingredients accordingly.

Consistency of the mixture: The glazing mixture you're going to apply on the surface of your pot should have a perfect consistency so that it is neither too thick not so thin. It should have a creamy and milky type of texture.

Glazing temperature: You need to be well acquainted with the temperature suitable for glazing. Too high or too low temperature is going to ruin your job.

Kiln: Being a beginner, you must know about the nature of the furnace. The temperature of your oven is crucial for your pottery work. Before beginning the firing process, you need to decide how much temperature you will set for your kiln. Also, be careful enough about the furnace, as you're going to get exposed in front of heat and fire, which is quite risky. Take the necessary safety measures before working with a kiln.

Celebrate your successes

When it comes to pottery, you want to celebrate your accomplishments. Did you manage to finally make the piece that has been giving you the worst experience ever? If that's the case, then take the time to celebrate it.

You definitely want to learn, but if you only focus on the faults, you'll definitely never get better. You also need to focus on the successes that you can get from this, and the different benefits that you can achieve from this.

Some things that you can do to celebrate your success are the following:

Give yourself a pat on the back or reward

Display the work somewhere and tell others about it

Consider selling it if you feel the pottery piece is extra-ordinary

Record the amazing feat that you did in a journal so that you know exactly what you did

Whatever the reason for your success might be, you should take the time to acknowledge something such as this. Pottery isn't something that you get right the first time, and if you're mastering a technique, it could take a little bit more time. But, if you work on this, better your skills, and take the time to work on the good things and master them, you'll be happy with your success.

Printed in Great Britain
by Amazon